Where the Light Enters

by Zohra Baqeri

Fomite
Burlington VT

ISBN-13: 978-1-967022-38-0
Library of Congress Control Number: 2026943097

Fomite
58 Peru Street
Burlington, VT 05401
www.fomitepress.com

05/28/2026

to my 14-year-old self

The wound is the place where the light enters you.

—Rumi

Contents

Dreams

Others live in their lives
But I live there.
Others think about their life
But I think about them.
Others want to go home
But I want to go there.
Others sleep to relax
But I sleep to go there.
My dreams are so beautiful
More than everything that exists in this world.
In your dreams you own your world, you live in your own world.
You can draw anything in your page of life's book.
You can write good things and bad things, that is up to you.
So try to have a good thing to write on your page.

(5 May 2024)

From the Time You Start to Live

From the time you start to live until the time you die, you learn new things.
It's the nature of humans to learn.
Your life doesn't start when you are born,
It starts when you really live it.
For living your life, you should know yourself, your world and your feelings.
Make your world the way you want.
No one can change your world but you.
It's never too late to change your world,
To start again.
Never destroy your world
Because from that time on the world tries to make you live
In the world you don't own,
Which is not from you.

(13 May 2024)

I See No Light

I see no light, outside of my mind.
My world is bigger than yours.
I create a world out of darkness.
You see, but I imagine.
I see a world more beautiful and bigger than what you see.
My imagination is more beautiful than what you see.
I have never seen the light, but the light inside me is lighter.
I imagine everything more beautiful than it really is.
I found my world inside the darkness.
I could make light in the darkness.
That's why I live in the light of my darkness.

(31 May 2024)

Walking Home from a Wedding

Hot day, high heels, long way home.

Step by step, faster and faster he was
following me. Fear taking up more
and more room inside me.

Fear became stress, stronger and stronger.
I stopped, looked back.
Nothing, except some old men walking slowly.

Strength replaced fear.
I walked on.
I heard the word *Shame*, looked at the man
I hadn't noticed walking beside me.

First I was upset by what he said.

But when I looked at him carefully, I realized that his
stress was stronger than mine. He was scared, shaking.

He quickly turned into another alley.
Soon I was feeling sorry and worried about him.

(31 May 2024)

It's Like There Are Two Souls

after Rumi

It's like there are two souls in one body.
It's like one is my heart and one is my mind
And I don't know what to do.

Sometimes, when I find interest in new things inside myself,
I think I was born like that.
It's like sometimes I think I was that person
but I was in the wrong place. Right feelings but wrong place.
I just realized it but I realized that you realized it a long time ago.
All your poems say it.
Just live to get to know yourself.
Live your life and don't try to be someone else.

(11 June 2024)

Is It Life?

A desk for work, work for a bed, a bed for sleep, sleep for a body, a body for death, a death for a memory, a memory for stone, is that life?

(11 June 2024)

My Window Doesn't Show Me Beauty

I don't want to watch outside
I pull the curtain
No light
No room
No window

Just a dark prison

Outside!
There is no light
Despite the brightness of the sun
Instead of red roses of hope
There are guns in men's hands

I'm afraid of them
I live in a place where I'm called infidel
And people must kill me to go to heaven
Those people think they are given life in order to kill us
To serve God!
I have to hide to survive

I'm breathing in a poisonous air and it's killing me
I'm that eagle that has to pretend to be a chicken
I have the dream of flying
But I have to hide my wings

God created me free!
Happy!
And proud
No one can take the rights which I have been given by God
They don't let women spread their wings
A woman is someone who wants to fly

I need to be called a woman in order to be a woman

I'm a girl
I'm a Hazara
I'm proud
and I will survive to prove it to people who don't know!

Notes:
A symbol of peace in Afghanistan is a white bird with a red rose.

Afghan fable: An eagle grew up with chickens and it could not fly. Whenever he saw an eagle in the sky, it wondered how the eagle got to be so powerful. The eagle with the chickens never learned to fly.

(16 July 2024)

The Song

the dancer must dance to be happy
even when she is forbidden
even when there is no song

it is not because her job is to dance
but because she is in love with dancing

some call her crazy, they do not see her love,
they do not see her dream

I understand the dancer
I am a student

my love is knowledge

a person without knowledge
is like a dancer without a song

(20 November 2024)

A Little Fire in My Room

The sound of water dropping from melting snow was like a melody
In my ears, like the jingling sound of a mobile when I was a baby
Or like the little bell on my black cat's neck
Or even the disturbance of the 5:00 a.m. ringtone

The sunshine's dance felt too good on my skin
The sky was so blue and bright that it was hard to believe
It was ever dark
The sun fooled us all with her hibernation
But here we are in a windy cold day disturbed by the sun
I'm sure I don't need a little fire in my room to fight the wild wind alone

(21 February 2024)

Spring

Long yawns wake up the world
Snow gives way to rain
Fountains leap to meet the rain
Finally, blooms dare to come out

Kites paint the sky
Flowers paint the ground
Carpets paint the roofs
And bird songs paint my heart

(20 April 2025)

I Come to the Shore of Death

I come to the shore of death
It is a giant ocean
But I can see heaven on the other side
I can hear the peaceful silence
I have to jump from the cliff
And drown
To reach it

Everything has a price
Even heaven requires death

(5 May 2025)

I Don't Like Pain

I don't like pain
It is too much
Then you get used to it
You don't feel it
Not feeling it is more painful
Like it's always with you

I think this time the stone went too deep
It has sunk my heart
My soul can cure me
But what can cure my soul?
Not any other soul knows about mine
Does it always have to suffer
Without anyone noticing?

I feel so deep
Deep down, someone's screaming
But no one hears it because it's too far down
Upper shields are smothering it

Those shields are torn now
But the scream is still so faint

Maybe it has gotten used to being ignored

(22 June 2025)

The Angel and the Devil

What would it be like to realize the angel was actually a devil
Bad was actually good
And what you call yourself is wrong
Who made (angel) sound good
And (devil) sound bad?
You were taught wrong all your life
Your life was an abuse of life
The silence of darkness was peace
And brightness of light blinded you

Then... you realize why the devil is no longer an angel
Maybe he knows better

(27 June 2025)

Don't Look at My Face, It's Ugly

Don't look at my face, it's ugly
Don't look at my smiles, they lie
Don't look at my eyes,
They are hiding pain
Don't look at my age,
It's not a lot

Don't look at my soul,
It's broken
Just ignore me as you have always done

If you remember me someday
Just remember a little girl with a pretty smile

(9 July 2025)

Ocean

What if the ocean is too enormous to cross?
Will you be brave enough to swim through
or just let yourself drown?

What if the land is overrun by wolves?

(9 July 2025)

Growth

Hearing giving up was for weak people
"Never fail" in my head
I had the people's support in my back

But the world opened my eyes

All the support was nothing but the fiction
That a little girl made for herself to feel safe

I gave up.
Not willing to take another breath of this toxic air
I dove into water

Now I understand that giving up is not always weakness
It's for peace

(13 July 2025)

I Am Still Here

I was born beneath a quiet sky
Where dreams were soft and eyes would cry,
Where silence grew inside my chest
And fear would steal my need for rest.

They called me weak, they called me wrong,
But still I learned to carry on.
I hid my hopes beneath my skin
And let the world bruise what's within.

I wanted books, not cages locked.
I wanted school, not doors that blocked.
I dreamed of helping girls like me
But chains were dressed as family.

My voice was small, but never gone,
Even when I whispered on.
Even when the nights were long,
Even when I doubted I belonged.

They say I'm nothing, blame my name,
But I have never played their game.
I wear my pain like hidden lace,
I carry stars behind my face.

I do not scream, but still I fight
In every thought I hold at night.
In every dream I dare to keep,
In every tear I've cried to sleep.

And now they say, "Don't go too far,"
Afraid I'll shine just like a star.

Afraid I'll live. Afraid I'll speak.
Afraid that quiet girls aren't weak.

But I am not their shadowed fear,
I am the light they tried to smear.
And though I'm bruised, and though I bend —
I will protect. I will defend.

I'll build a life they said I couldn't,
Love myself when they said I shouldn't.
And one day girls will say my name
Not with sorrow — but with flame.

(18 July 2025)

Where the Light Enters

In the quiet after storm, light fades,
Where silence hums and pain once stayed,
A tender bud begins to rise—
A whisper blooming toward the skies.

Not all wounds bleed where eyes can see,
Some ache in places meant to be
Soft gardens, warm with love and trust—
Now cracked with sorrow, curled in dust.

But healing isn't loud or fast,
It doesn't chase away the past.
It sits with you when nights feel cold,
And gives your trembling, hands to hold.

It speaks in breaths, in tears let free,
In learning that it's safe to be
Exactly who you are inside,
With nothing left to shrink or hide.

You are not broken, only bruised,
Not something lost, but being used
To carve a path through darkened days,
Toward softer thoughts and gentler ways.

Each scar a map, each tear a seed,
Each moment still, just what you need.
And slowly, like the dawn's first hue
The world turns gold, and so do you.

(24 July 2025)

We Are All Victims

Victims of sick minds.

Prisoners of fear,
Rotting in dark prisons.

Endless darkness,
An infinite gloom of diseased thoughts.

I have always laughed in my prison,
Danced, cried.

But the heavy chains have shown no mercy
To the delicate body of a little girl.

The chains were golden—made of "closeness," "responsibility," "love,"
Linked to the shining name of family.

The chains tightened around my throat
But I laughed,
Laughed at the power of oppressive lies,
At the power of love and responsibility imposed by force.

Every time I tried to fly
The chains pulled me down.

I tried to break the chains.

They got scared and bound me tighter
With a new link: "shame."

They crush me to the ground
And I cannot stand.

(6 August 2025)

A Girl Cries

A girl cries
Not for her scars but for her rights.
You can burn her wings
But she can grow them bigger
This time
Maybe you can make her wear burqa
But you cannot hide what she has
Under it maybe her mind's brightness
Blocks your sight

But you can't hide the sun with two fingers

(9 August 2025)

Darkness

I sing to keep the dark away

The darkness threatening my soul
Whispering behind my ear softly

The poisonous words of love
Winning my immature heart

I hate this darkness
I hate how unavoidable it is

(9 September 2025)

Bruised Wings

I dreamed big—believing I was special, believing I could make it.

But the truth broke open like a sharp wind, tearing me apart.

In the wide, dark ocean of my mind
I am struggling to stay afloat, drowning under fears.

I thought I was Cinderella, but I never had a fairy to grant my wish.
They told me to dream high—so I rose as high as I could,
not knowing my wings weren't ready to fly.

And now my wings are bruised,
aching with every memory of how far I fell.

And now I'm terrified—terrified that my dreams
were only daydreams, fragile as smoke.

Afraid to wish, afraid to hope; my dreams feel heavier now,
more burden than blessing.

I was the black sheep among fair, lovely ewes—
but their wool was never as white as they pretended.

Their warmth was a lie, their closeness a shadow;
and the betrayal still stings like cold air against open skin.

Yet even now, even bruised, even shaken,
a small part of me still lifts its face to the sky—
still wishing, still hoping, still wanting to fly.

(27 November 2025)

Quiet Below the Streets

We walked a Kabul afternoon,
my mother's hand warm in mine—
a simple moment,
a quiet breath.

Then shadows gathered,
not shouting,
just closing in
like heavy thoughts do
on difficult days.

They took us where
the streets grew narrow,
where sunlight folded
into quiet corners,
where steps echoed
with old fears.

The path turned bending,
turning
soft and strange—
a maze made of
everything I worry about
but never say aloud.

And somewhere
between one turn and the next,
my mother faded
like a whispered name—
and I felt the small ache
of being suddenly alone.

A room waited at the end,
bright, silent,
too clean to feel alive.
People spoke of roles
I never wanted,
weights I could not carry,
choices that weren't mine.

But inside me
a gentler voice—
small, trembling,
but true—
rose like a candle
in a still room.

I do not belong here.

And the dream loosened.
Fear thinned.
Light found its way back
through the cracks.

I woke knowing
the dream wasn't a prophecy—
only a reflection
of how deeply I have been brave,
how much I have held in silence,
how strong I remain
even when I feel fragile.

(27 November 2025)

Little Joy

The sun found my face today, and I smiled without a reason.
For a moment, everything felt light—
like my heart remembered how to fly.

(15 December 2025)

What Do You Call a Flower Before It Becomes a Flower?

When I am quiet on the surface,
there is a poem growing deep inside,

A poem is just some words springing from a random little feeling
that is keeping you quiet.

(22 December 2025)

Quiet Girl

She was a quiet girl, the kind who learned early
that silence kept rooms calmer.

A hand would rise—not loud, not sudden, just heavy with permission.
And she stood still, like stillness was a rule written into her bones.

Words cut deeper than the sound ever could.
"Behave."
"Endure."
"Perfect girls don't complain."

Chains weren't iron—they were expectations, tight smiles,
the way her throat closed every time she wanted to scream.

When her voice trembled, they scolded the tremble.
When her eyes filled, they called it weakness.

So she learned the art of swallowing storms.
Anger folded small.
Pain packed neatly away.
Dreams pressed flat until they barely took up space.

She carried everything inside—because she was taught
that perfection meant never spilling, never breaking,
never asking to be held.

And still—beneath the quiet, beneath the chains—something breathed.

Not loud.
Not free.

But alive,

Waiting.

(26 December 2025)

About the Author

A teenage girl with a heart full of poems and quiet dreams. She finds comfort in music, peace in silence, and beauty in the sound of nature. Most days, she writes what she can not say out loud. Somewhere in her heart lives a simple dream of one day learning to ride her bike through green mountain roads.

Writing a review on social media sites for readers will help the progress of independent publishing. To submit a review, go to the book page on any of the sites and follow the links for reviews. Books from independent presses rely on reader-to-reader communications.

For more information or to order any of our books, visit:

http://www.fomitepress.com/our-books.html

More poetry from Fomite...

Warren Baker
Shadow Light
Anna Blackmer
Hexagrams
L. Brown
Loopholes
Sue D. Burton
Little Steel
Christine Butterworth-McDermott
Evelyn As
The Spellbook of Fruit and Flowers
David Cavanagh
Cycling in Plato's Cave
Please Hold
Rajnesh Chakrapani
The Repetition of Exceptional Weeks
James Connolly
Picking Up the Bodies
Benjamin Dangl
A World Where Many Worlds Fit
Greg Delanty
Behold the Garden
Loosestrife
Mason Drukman
Drawing on Life
J. C. Ellefson
Foreign Tales of Exemplum and Woe

Anna Faktorovich

Improvisational Arguments

Peter Fortunato

World Headquarters

Barry Goldensohn

Snake in the Spine, Wolf in the Heart

The Hundred Yard Dash Man

The Listener Aspires to the Condition of Music

Visitors Entrance

Lorrie Goldensohn

Little Fish

R. L. Green

When You Remember Deir Yassin

KJ Hannah Greenberg

Beast There—Don't That

Kevin Hadduck

Beloved Brother, Beloved Sister

John Hawkins

Mirror to Mirror

Christopher Heffernan

[laughter]

Gail Holst-Warhaft

Lucky Country

Judith Kerman

Definitions

Yahia Lababidi

Quarantine Notes

Joseph Lamport

Enlightenment

Raymond Luczak

A Babble of Objects

Kate Magill

Roadworthy Creature, Roadworthy Craft

Tony Magistrale
Entanglements
Gary Mesick
General Discharge
Giorigio Mobili
Sunken Boulevards
Andreas Nolte
Mascha: The Poems of Mascha Kaléko
Sherry Olson
Four-Way Stop
Brett Ortler
Lessons of the Dead
David Polk
Drinking the River
Janice Miller Potter
Meanwell
Thoreau's Umbrella
Philip Ramp
Arrivals and Departures
The Melancholy of a Life as the Joy of Living It Slowly Chills
Joseph D. Reich
A Case Study of Werewolves
Connecting the Dots to Shangrila
The Derivation of Cowboys and Indians
The Hole That Runs Through Utopia
The Housing Market
Kenneth Rosen and Richard Wilson
Gomorrah
Fred Rosenblum
Of Our Elaborate Plans
Playing Chicken with an Iron Horse
Tramping Solo
Vietnumb

David Schein
  My Murder and Other Local News
Harold Schweizer
  Miriam's Book
Scott T. Starbuck
  Carbonfish Blues
  Hawk on Wire
  Industrial Oz
Seth Steinzor
  Among the Lost
  Once Was Lost
  To Join the Lost
  The Dragon of Sassafras Mountain
Susan Thomas
  In the Sadness Museum
  Silent Acts of Public Indiscretion
  The Empty Notebook Interrogates Itself
Sharon Webster
  Everyone Lives Here
  O Song
Tony Whedon
  The Tres Riches Heures
  The Falkland Quartet
Claire Zoghb
  Dispatches from Everest

More dual language titles from Fomite

Vito Bonito/Alison Grimaldi Donahue
  Soffiata Via/Blown Away
Antonello Borra
  Erbario/lapidario
Antonello Borra/Blossom Kirschenbaum
  Alfabestiario
  AlphaBetaBestiaro

Antonello Borra/Anis Memon
Fabbrica delle idee/The Factory of Ideas
Alessio Brandolini/Giorgio Mobili
Miniature Cities
Lorenzo Carlucci/Todd Portnowitz
Methods
Jeannette Clariond/Lawrence Schimel
Desert Memory
Silvia Comoglio/Giorgio Mobili
Via Crucis
Tina Escaja/Mark Eisner
Caída Libre/Free Fall
Luigi Fontanella/Giorgio Mobili
L'Adolescenza e la notte/Adolescence and Night
JohannesHösle/Marc Estrin
Album aus Dietenbronn/Whatever Befalls
Aristea Papalexandrou/Philip Ramp
Μας προσπερνά/It's Overtaking Us
Katerina Anghelaki-Rooke/Philip Ramp
Losing Appetite for Existence
Mikis Theodoraksi/Gail Holst-Warhaft
The House with the Scorpions
Paolo Valesio/Todd Portnowitz
La Mezzanotte di Spoleto/Midnight in Spoleto

www.ingramcontent.com/pod-product-compliance
Lightning Source LLC
Chambersburg PA
CBHW021348060726
47591CB00006B/2210

* 9 7 8 1 9 6 7 0 2 2 3 8 0 *